# The Plum Trip

Written by Teresa Heapy

Illustrated by Jan Smith

## Collins

Spot and Sambar went on a trip to pick plums.

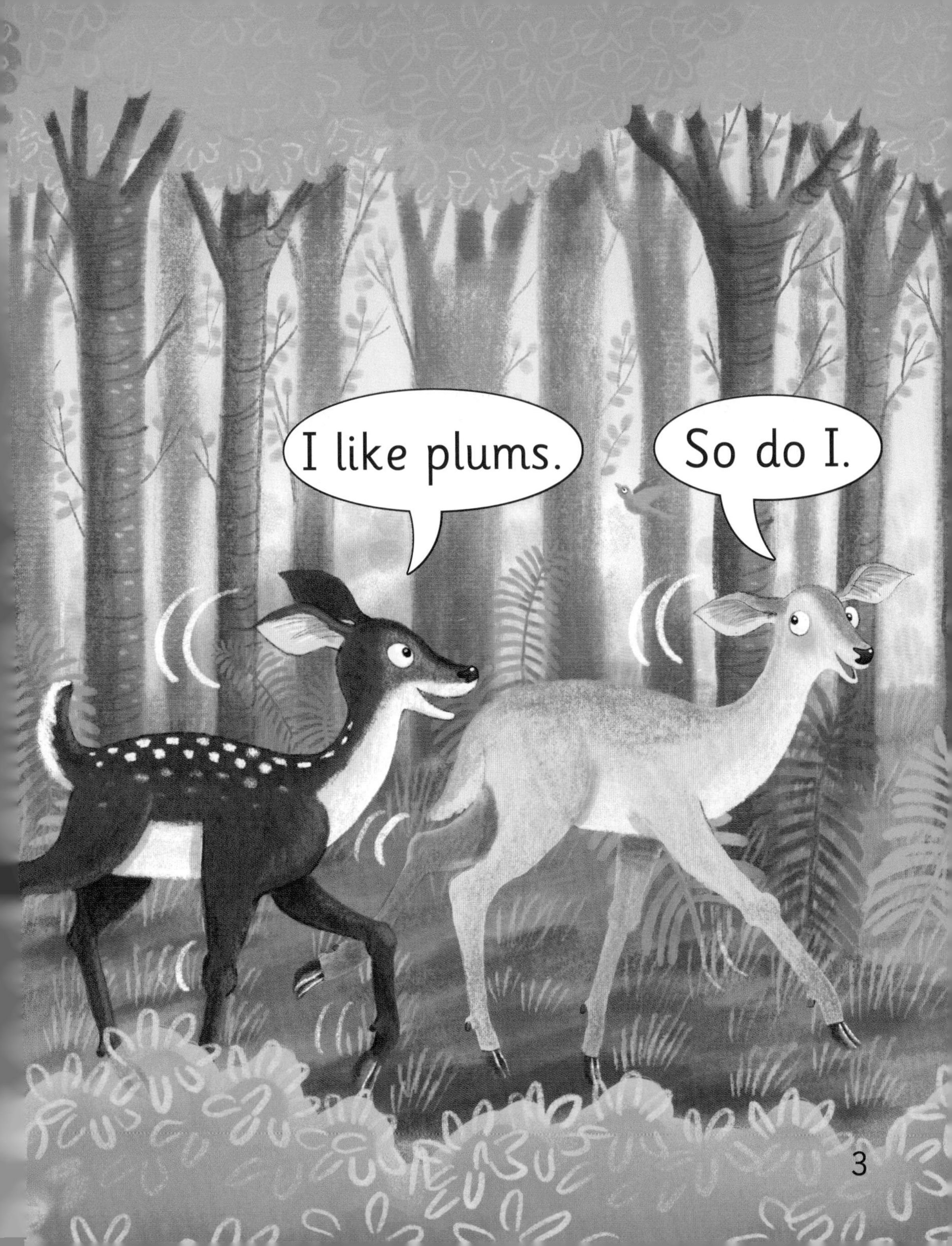
I like plums.
So do I.

"This is the best spot for plums!"
said Sambar.

"We must jump to get them!"
said Spot.

There was lots of mud.

slip

skid

slam

"I have a plan, Spot," said Sambar.

"Stand here," Sambar said.
Spot waited.

Sambar got on his back.

Spot felt a little ant on his leg.

Sambar landed on Spot.

The plums landed on Sambar and Spot.

slip

slop

slap

splat

Spot and Sambar sat up.

We got some plums!

# Plum trip

**Letters and Sounds:** Phase 4

**Word count:** 101

Focus on adjacent consonants with short vowel phonemes, e.g. *trip*.

**Common exception words:** to, the, I, we, was, said, have, like, so, do, some, there, little, of, here

**Curriculum links:** Understanding the world

**Curriculum links (National Curriculum, Year 1):** Science: Animals, including humans

**Early learning goals:** Reading: read and understand simple sentences; use phonic knowledge to decode regular words and read them aloud accurately; read some common irregular words; demonstrate understanding when talking with others about what they have read.

**National Curriculum learning objectives:** Reading/word reading: read accurately by blending sounds in unfamiliar words containing GPCs that have been taught; Reading/comprehension: understand both the books they can already read accurately and fluently and those they listen to by checking that the text makes sense to them as they read, and correcting inaccurate reading

## Developing fluency

- Encourage your child to follow the words as you read the first pages with expression.
- Take turns to read a page, encouraging your child to read the spoken words and speech bubbles in a voice that matches the characters. Ensure they don't miss the speech bubbles and action words.

## Phonic practice

- Practise reading words that contain adjacent consonants. Encourage your child to sound out and blend the following:
  plums    slop    splat    stand
- Challenge your child to sound out the following words with more than one syllable:
  Sam-bar    land-ed    wait-ed

## Extending vocabulary

- Reread page 6 and discuss why the deer are skidding on the mud. Can your child think of words to describe mud? (e.g. *sloppy, slimy, skiddy, gooey*)
- Look at page 13 and challenge your child to suggest words that describe how the plums might taste. (e.g. *sweet, juicy, yummy*)